Hiking in the Hills

By Cameron Macintosh

AF585338

Hiking can be great fun.
You can hike along the coast or
in the bush.

Have you ever hiked in the hills?

Kate has hiked a lot, so she's very skilled.

Kate and Mum take this sloping track.
Kate loves gazing out across the landscape.

Tim and Dad take a safer track because Tim has not hiked a lot.

This track is flatter and shaded by trees.

Jack likes using poles when he's hiking so he does not fall.

Yousef likes taking photos while he's hiking in the hills.

He thinks taking photos on film is nicer than taking digital photos! He prints his photos and gets them framed.

film

Sam and Dad like hiking as the sun is rising.

Today, they timed their hike just right!

Nan and Pip the dog love hiking
when the sun is up and shining!

Branko used to not like hiking. He changed his mind because he likes to see animals.

It is much nicer to see animals in the wild.

Branko gaped when he saw this animal!
It's the largest animal he has seen in the wild.

Kelly's bush group is hiking in the hills.

Kelly would like a rest, but she's still smiling!
With each step, she gets closer to the top!

Pom loves coming along on hikes. She is having fun running in the mud!

Would you like to go hiking in the hills?

Pom is hoping you will take her along!

CHECKING FOR MEANING

1. Why is Kate very skilled at hiking? *(Literal)*
2. What does Yousef like to do while he is hiking? *(Literal)*
3. Does Kelly enjoy hiking? How do you know? *(Inferential)*
4. What do you think would be the best time of day to hike in the hills? Why? *(Evaluative)*

EXTENDING VOCABULARY

sloping	What does a sloping track look like? What is the opposite of a sloping track? What word in the text is related to this opposite word?
shaded	What is the base of the word *shaded*? What would create shade on a track in the hills?
largest	What is the base of the word *largest*? How does adding the suffix *est* change the meaning of the word *large*?

MOVING BEYOND THE TEXT

1. Where would you like to go for a walk or a hike?
2. What might be hard about hiking?
3. What animals or plants might you see on a hike near where you live?
4. Some people take photos with their phone and some people use a digital camera or a film camera. Do you like taking photos? What do you use to take photos?

TIME TO WRITE

Write about what you might see on a hike near your home.